HOW
ANY KID
CAN START
A BUSINESS

How Any Kid Can Start a Business

Published by Matcha360 LLC, 11700 W. Charleston Boulevard #170-469, Las Vegas, Nevada 89135

For permissions to reprint, contact Matcha360 LLC by mail at 11700 W. Charleston Boulevard #170-469, Las Vegas, Nevada 89135, or electronically at Ian@HowAnyKidCanStartABusiness.com.

About the Authors

Mark Cuban

Since the age of 12, Mark has been a natural entrepreneur. Selling garbage bags door to door, the seed was planted early on for what would eventually become long-term success. Cuban is now an American billionaire businessman, investor, film producer, author, television personality, philanthropist, and serial entrepreneur. He is the owner of the NBA's Dallas Mavericks, Landmark Theaters, and Magnolia Pictures, and the chairman of AXS TV. He is also a "shark" investor on ABC's hit primetime television show *Shark Tank*. Cuban is also the author of the bestseller *How To Win At The Sport of Business*.

Shaan Patel

Shaan has always been an entrepreneur at heart. In elementary school, he sold Pokemon cards. In middle school, he sold music CDs. In high school, he made thousands off internet referrals. In college, he made tens of thousands selling used iPhones on eBay. After achieving a perfect score on the SAT, Shaan found his real business: Prep Expert—a test prep company offering SAT & ACT prep classes in twenty cities and online. Shaan appeared on *Shark Tank* to pitch Prep Expert and closed an investment deal with Mark Cuban. Patel is also author of multiple bestselling SAT & ACT prep books.

Ian McCue

Ian is the founder and director of Spark Skill, an educational startup offering coding, design, and maker summer camps for tweens and teens. At just 16-years old, he is an entrepreneur with extensive experience in STEM and educational ventures, along with a passion for promoting youth engagement in coding, engineering, and business development.

Letter from the Authors

Welcome! Every day, parents and their kids ask us for ideas on what kinds of businesses kids can start and run. Believe it or not, there are plenty of businesses that kids as young as 8 or 9 years old can start doing! Running a lemonade stand for a few hours is a great experience. However, there are so many more ways for a kid to not only gain valuable experience in the business world, but to earn some extra money as well.

We hope our book, *How Any Kid Can Start a Business*, will give kids a great head start to launching their own age-appropriate business.

Let us know your thoughts by emailing us at

feedback@HowAnyKidCanStartABusiness.com

Mark, Shaan, and Ian

TABLE OF CONTENTS

INTRODUCTION

WHAT IS
AN ENTREPRENEUR?

WHAT DO YOU WANT TO BE WHEN YOU GROW UP?

Have you ever been asked, "What do you want to be when you grow up?" Most kids reply with the following:

"I want to be a doctor."

"I want to be a firefighter."

"I want to be an engineer."

But have you ever heard someone say, "I want to be an entrepreneur"? Probably not. That's because most people don't know what an entrepreneur is. An entrepreneur is a person who starts a business to make money. This book is really about entrepreneurship. Any kid who starts a business to make money is an entrepreneur.

how to pronounce
entrepreneur:
on-truh-pren-yur

So, the next time you are asked what you want to be when you grow up, you can say, "I want to be an entrepreneur!"

Another word for anyone who starts a business is "founder." If you start a business called "Sweeties Lemonade Stand," then you are the founder of the Sweeties Lemonade Stand. So when you start a business, you can call yourself both an entrepreneur and a founder.

While the authors of this book are now successful entrepreneurs and our companies have made millions of dollars, we all started as kid entrepreneurs first. Mark Cuban started by selling garbage bags door-to-door to neighbors as his first business. Shaan Patel started by selling Pokemon cards to his friends in elementary school as his first business. Ian McCue started by selling websites as his first business.

By starting a simple business as a kid, you will learn more about entrepreneurship than any class could ever teach you. You will learn about sales, costs, hard work, and more. But you have to get started by starting a business, even if it's as simple as opening a lemonade stand. If we can do it, you can do it.

THE GOAL OF ENTREPRENEURSHIP

So, what is entrepreneurship all about? While most kids think that business is about making money, money is only one side of it. The end goal of any business is to help people.

You can help by doing something useful, important, or good for other people. The goal of business should be to help other people by making their lives just a little bit better.

A successful business must help people in some way. If you're looking to both make money and help people, then business is for you.

Business is about building something great that you love. There is nothing more fun and fulfilling. If you care about your idea and are willing to work hard, become an entrepreneur by starting a business.

HELP PEOPLE +
MAKE MONEY
=
BUSINESS

DISCOVERING
YOUR BUSINESS IDEA

IMPROVE LIFE
ONE CUP OF LEMONADE AT A TIME

You now know what entrepreneurship is, and how an entrepreneur can succeed. Let's start identifying some business ideas! Every successful business is built on a simple idea that makes life better. This improvement can be tiny, yet still change the world!

What could you do to make life a little bit better?

Our business ideas in this book include washing cars, selling home goods, and making unique shoelaces. So, how do these improve life?

❋ Washing cars: keeps cars looking fresh

❋ Selling home goods: reduces time spent shopping and saves customers' money

❋ Seling unique shoelaces: adds a pop of fun to any pair of shoes

How would the next three ideas improve life?

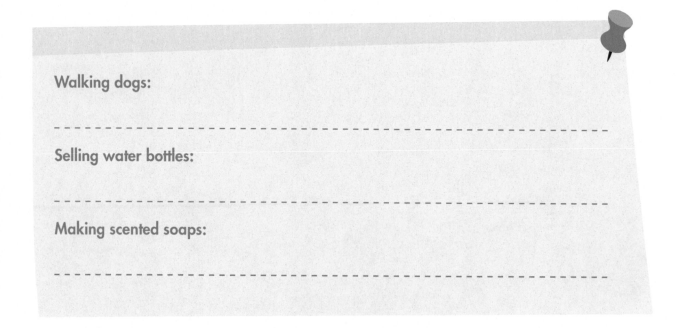

Walking dogs:

- -

Selling water bottles:

- -

Making scented soaps:

- -

Even simple ideas can make life better. So, how do you come up with your own ideas, and how do you choose one? Let's dive in.

14

DISCOVERING YOUR OWN IDEAS

What products or services could improve your life? Think through your day from start to finish. Did you do any chores that you could have paid someone else to do? What could have been improved?

When you try to come up with a list of business ideas, follow these two steps:

1. Find a problem, no matter how small, in your daily life.

2. Come up with a product or service that could solve this problem.

Here are the steps for three of our business ideas:

Washing cars

1. My parents have to go to the car wash often. It costs $10, and it takes so long.

2. I could take the $10 that they pay, wash their cars myself, and save them time and effort.

Selling home goods

1. Buying trash bags and other essentials at grocery stores in small numbers is convenient, but expensive.

2. I could buy large numbers of these products at cheaper stores, and then sell them for more in my neighborhood. My customers would save money, and I would make money.

Selling unique shoelaces

1. My old shoes could use a pop of color. I'd love to support my school's sports team, too.

2. I could buy shoe laces that match my school colors. My shoes would look as good as new!

Write the steps that you could have taken to discover these ideas:

Walking dogs:

1. _____

2. _____

Selling water bottles:

1. _____

2. _____

Making scented soaps:

1. _____

2. _____

Now, come up with three of your own ideas by following the steps:

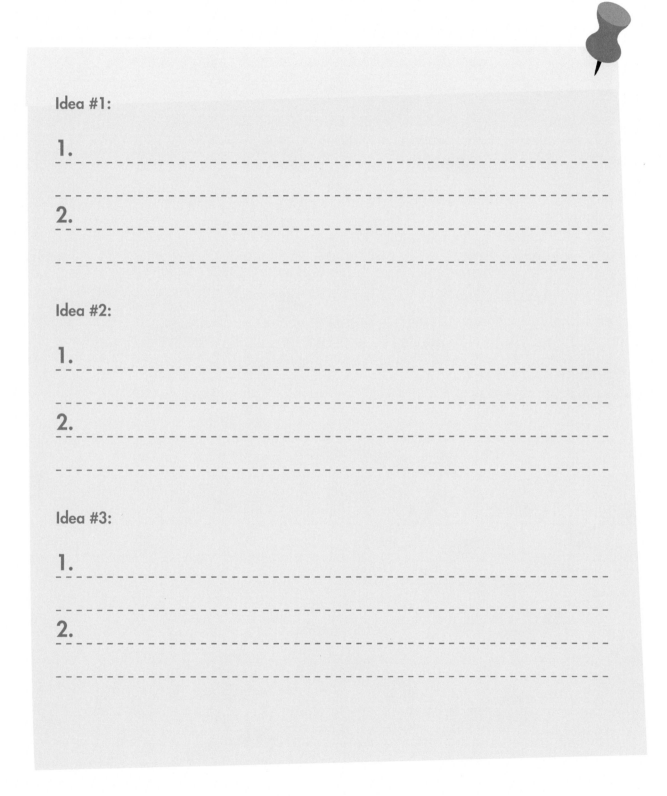

Idea #1:

1. _____

2. _____

Idea #2:

1. _____

2. _____

Idea #3:

1. _____

2. _____

SELECTING
THE WINNER

Not all ideas will make a good business. Some can become million-dollar companies, and others can't. Some are expensive to start, and others can be started for free. So, how do you pick an idea?

You may be surprised that you should not pick the idea that could make you the most money, or the idea that would cost you the least. Instead, you should pick the idea that **you will be best at**, and that you will **work the hardest at**. If you aren't talented or skilled at something, it is not a good idea to start a business doing it. If you aren't willing to work hard on a business idea, it isn't for you.

Other than that, it's up to you! If you have many ideas that you are good at and will work hard at, talk to your friends and family to hear their opinions. Maybe they see you as even more talented at something than you think you are!

10 BUSINESSES
ANY KID CAN START

1 SCENTED SOAPS

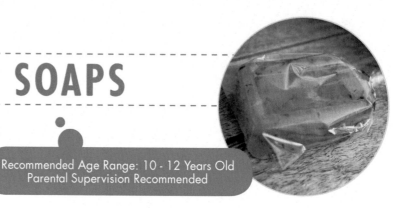

Recommended Age Range: 10 - 12 Years Old
Parental Supervision Recommended

Materials & Costs

Microwave Safe Bowl — —

Spatula or Mixing Utensil — —

20 Small Bars with Recommended Kit: $1 / Soap Bar
Everything Lavender Soap Making Kit By
ArtMinds™ (*Included in Kit:* · Base · Color ·
Flowers · Fragrance)

Additional Required Items: $0.05 / Soap Bar
Bags with Ties

Total Cost: **$1.05** per Soap Bar

Sale Price

$3 — **$5**
One Two

Revenue: **$3 to $5** per Sale

SALES STRATEGY

Bundle Goods

Reduce your price per item when people buy
more of them. In this business, you will profit $2
if you sell one bar, or $3 if you sell two bars.

People will be more likely to purchase two bars
because of the lower price per bar of soap.

One bar: $3 - $1.05 = **$1.95** of Profit
Two bars: $5 - $2.10 = **$2.90** of Profit

MAKE IT! A Visual How-To Guide

A Place half of the soap in a micro-wave-safe bowl and, with a parent's assistance, microwave it in 30 second intervals until melted.

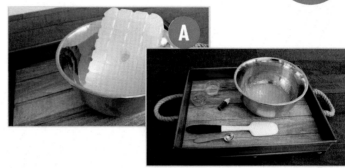

B Add one drop of color, two drops of fragrance, and a large sprinkle of Lavender Flowers and mix.

C Pour the complete mix carefully into your molds, filling them halfway. Wait an hour, then remove and individually wrap in clear bags.

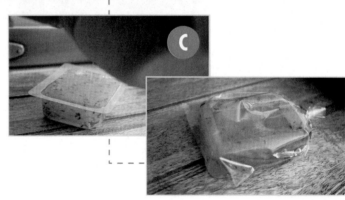

SELL IT!

Etsy

Sell your soaps on the largest online handmade goods store! Visit **Etsy.com** to learn how.

Farmer's Market

Set up shop in a local farmer's market to have your customers come to you! Find a regular, local market near you, bring some samples, and spend a day talking to their customers and sellers about your business. They will likely have excellent advice for your product, sales, and local laws that could apply.

2 DUCT TAPE WALLETS

Recommended Age Range: 7 - 9 Years Old

Lightweight Wallets

Almost everyone has a wallet, but most wallets are far too bulky and bland. These easy-to-make duct tape wallets are easy to customize, and will make a great profit for you.

Price Range

$5 Low $8 Ideal $10 High

Revenue: **$8** per wallet

Materials & Cost

Ruler & Scissors	—
Duct Tape	$0.50 / wallet

Cost: **$0.50** per wallet

$8 - $0.50 = **$7.50** of Profit per Wallet

MAKE IT! A Visual How-To Guide

A Prepare your materials. We will refer to our black duct tape as the main tape, and our silver duct tape as the style tape. Feel free to use whatever colors of tape you would like on each step!

B Cut four pieces of your tape to be eight inches long each.

C Overlap each piece of tape by half of an inch.

D Repeat steps B and C using the style tape.

E Stack the two rectangles on top of each other, sticky sides together. Start from one side and work your way to the other to reduce air bubbles.

F Cut a ten-inch piece of style tape in in half lengthwise so that it is long and thin. Take one half and fold it over the top of the rectangle. Take the other half and fold it over the bottom. Trim the edges.

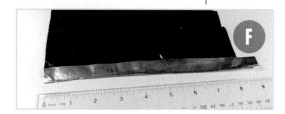

G Fold the rectangle in half as shown. Cut two pieces of style tape to be three inches long. Carefully fold them around each side of the wallet.

H Trim the excess tape.

23

I Cut two pieces of primary tape to be slightly longer than the wallet. Carefully and fully overlap these pieces to make a pocket.

J Cut two pieces of style tape two inches long. Carefully align them to either side of the newly added pocket, and fold them over, attaching the pocket's sides to the wallet.

K Cut another piece of style tape to be slightly longer than the wallet. Rest the bottom of the wallet on the middle of the tape. Fold the tape over, sealing the bottom. Remove excess from the sides.

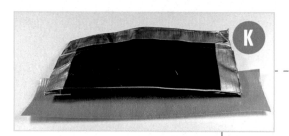

L Trim a piece of style tape to be slightly taller than the wallet. Cut it in half lengthwise, making it long and thin. Carefully align it with the middle of the pocket, place it, and then fold the excess into the interior of the wallet.

M Make more! Try mixing up the colors of duct tape.

SELL IT!

Door to Door

Go from one house to the next with your parent and a few of your wallets. Knock on the door, and start with something like this: "Hi, I'm ____! Would you be interested in a lightweight Duct Tape Wallet?

Social Media

Ask your friends and family to share your wallets on Facebook and Instagram. Send them a picture of the wallet with your phone number or email address in the background as seen above.

3 HOME GOODS

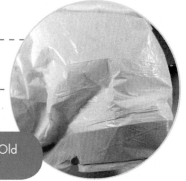

Recommended Age Range: 7 - 9 Years Old
Parental Supervision Recommended

Sale Price

$2 **$3**

Ten Bags   Twenty Bags

Revenue: **$2 to $3** per Sale

Materials & Costs

Trash Bags $0.10 / Bag

Cost: **$0.10** per Bag

Ten Bags: $2 - (10 x $0.10) = **$1.00** of Profit
Twenty Bags: $3 - (20 x $0.10) = **$1.00** of Profit

SELL IT!

Door to Door

Go from one house to the next with your parent and a couple of large boxes of trash bags. Knock on the door, and start with something like this: "Hi, does your family use garbage bags?" If they start to object, say, "Of course you use garbage bags, and I bet you pay more than fifteen cents a piece." (This sales strategy is from Mark Cuban's *First Entrepreneurial Venture*)

4 WATER BOTTLES

Recommended Age Range: 10 - 12 Years Old
Parental Supervision Recommended

Materials & Costs

Large Cooler	—	
Ice for Cooler	$0.05 / Bottle	
Water Bottles	$0.20 / Bottle	

Cost per Bottle: $0.25

Sale Price

$1 1 Bottle

Revenue: $1 per Sale

$1 - $0.25 = **$0.75** of Profit per Bottle

SELL IT!

High Traffic Events

Set up a small stand at a local youth event sports game (with permission from the location). The number of potential customers is a great boost to business!

Choose a hot day outdoors in a place with lots of foot traffic for killer sales!

Walking Trails and Parks

Walk around your local trails or parks and offer your cold water bottles to people for just $1. Although these locations have fewer people, it is often easier to get permission to set up shop.

5 LEMONADE

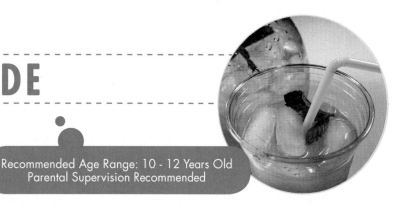

Recommended Age Range: 10 - 12 Years Old
Parental Supervision Recommended

Materials & Costs

 Large Pitcher —

 Mixing Tool —

 Mug or Coffee Cup —

Hot Filtered Water —

 Standard Measuring Cups —

 Half a Cup of Sugar $1.00 / Pitcher

Half a Cup of Lemon Juice $1.50 / Pitcher

 Two and a Half Cups of Filtered Water $0.05 / Pitcher

 Two and a Half Cups of Ice $0.05 / Pitcher

 Plastic Cups and Straws $0.05 / Cup

 Mint Leaves $0.05 / Cup

Cost per Pitcher: **$2.60** • Cups per Pitcher: **8** • Cost per Cup: **$0.43**

Sale Price

 $1   1 Cup - Ideal   Revenue: **$1** per Sale

$1 - $0.43 = **$0.57** of Profit per Cup

MAKE IT! A Visual How-to Guide

A Pour around half a cup of hot water into a mug or coffee cup, and immediately add half a cup of sugar. Mix to dissolve for three minutes.

B Pour half a cup of lemon juice, two and a half cups of filtered water, and the dissolved sugar into the pitcher. Mix briefly, then add two and a half cups of ice. Add a large branch of mint leaves for decoration.

C When someone purchases a cup, fill it, leaving an inch of space at the top. Add a mint leaf and a straw.

SELL IT!

High Traffic Events

Set up a small stand at a local youth event sports game (with permission from the location). The volume of potential customers is a great boost to business!

Social Media

Create a Facebook event for your lemonade stand. Have your friends and family share it and invite people to join!

6 CAR WASH CRAZE

Recommended Age Range: 10 - 12 Years Old
Parental Supervision Recommended

Materials & Costs

Sponges	—
Rags/Towels	—
Two Buckets of Water	—
Car Wash Soap	$1.00 / Car

Cost per Car: $1.00

Service Price

$9 Exterior Hand Wash

Revenue: $9 per Wash

$9 - $1 = **$8** of Profit per Wash

WASH IT! A Visual How-to Guide

A Add car wash soap as directed to one of the buckets of water. Place a sponge in each bucket of water.

B Rinse the outside of the car with the sponge from the bucket of clean, plain water.

C Use the sponge from the bucket of soapy water to scrub the car.

D Repeat step B.

E Use clean rags/towels to gently dry the outside of the car.

SELL IT!

Door to Door

Go from one house to the next with flyers for your service. Ring the doorbell. If they answer, briefly introduce yourself, saying, "Hi, I'm ____, the neighborhood car washer! Here is my contact information (hand them a flyer), and note that the first wash is free! Please let me know if I can ever be of assistance!"

Local Events

Set up a small stand at a gym or park (with permission from the location). People will be busy at the event, and it is an ideal time for them to get a car wash.

SALES STRATEGY

Free Trial

Offer a free car wash to potential repeat customers! If you do a great job, they are very likely to continue using your service on a regular basis. Reserve this offer for neighbors and friends.

7 NEIGHBORHOOD DOG WALKING

Recommended Age Range: 10 - 12 Years Old
Parental Supervision Recommended

Materials & Costs

 Two Dog Leashes —

Service Price

$10 **$15**
Half Hour   Full Hour

Revenue: $10 to $15 per Walk

Reducing Risk

In order to provide a quality service and reduce your risk, only walk as many dogs as you can realistically control. We recommend handling no more than two at a time. However, charge the same prices regardless of whether your customer has one or two dogs.

Selling Flexibility

Allow neighbors with one dog each to split the cost of you walking their dogs together. It is unlikely that their schedules will always match, so you will often still collect the full price from each happy customer. Make sure that their dogs are friendly to each other first.

Half Hour: $10 of Profit per Walk
Full Hour: $15 of Profit per Walk

SELL IT!

Door to Door

Go from one house to the next with flyers for your service. Ring the doorbell. If they answer, briefly introduce yourself, saying, "Hi, I'm _____, the neighborhood dog walker! Here is my contact information (hand them a flyer), and note that the first half hour walk is free! Please let me know if I can ever help!"

Social Media

List your job on Facebook as "Neighborhood Dog Walker." With owners' permission, post photos of you walking dogs every so often. This will help ensure that you stay fresh in the minds of potential customers.

SALES STRATEGY

Free Trial

Offer a free, half-hour walk to each potential customer! Once they see how happy their dog is, they are more likely to continue using your services.

8 UNIQUE SHOELACES

Recommended Age Range: 7 - 9 Years Old
Parental Supervision Recommended

Materials & Costs

Cotton Shoelaces $3 / Pair

Cost Per Shoelace: $3

Sale Price

$10   **$14**   **$19**

Low   Ideal   High

Revenue: $14 per Pair

$14 - $3 = **$11** of Profit per Pair of Shoelaces

SELL IT!

Etsy

Sell your shoelaces on the largest online handmade goods store! Visit Etsy.com today to learn how.

High Traffic Events

Set up a small stand at a local youth event sports game (with permission from the location). Sell lots of shoelaces that match the competing teams' colors. The volume of likely customers is a great boost to business!

SALES STRATEGY

Referral Marketing

Let your friends and peers work for you! Every time that someone you know finds a shoelace buyer for you, give them $3 of your profit on that sale. They will be motivated to help you as much as possible!

9 SENIOR TECH HELP

Recommended Age Range: 10 - 12 Years Old

Smartphone, Tablet, Computer, and Social Media Training and Troubleshooting

Service Price

$20 — **$30**

Half Hour   Full Hour

Revenue: $20 to $30

Capitalize on Your Skills

In order to provide a quality service, ask your client what they need before scheduling a time with them. This will allow you to better judge how long you will need, and to ensure that you know how to fix the issues that they need help with.

SELL IT!

Customers List

Talk to your friends and family and come up with a list of people who may be interested in your services. Determine what about your service will be valuable to them, write down what you will say, and then contact them (typically through email or phone). Note their response and what you learned from it.

Social Media

List your job on Facebook as "Senior Tech Help." Post photos with your clients (and their approval) every so often. This will help make sure that you stay fresh in the minds of potential customers.

10 SNOW SHOVELING

Recommended Age Range: 10 - 12 Years Old
Parental Supervision Recommended

Materials & Costs

Snow Shovel   —

Service Price

$20
First Half Hour

$10
Every Additional
Half Hour

Revenue: $20 +

Snow Shoveling Tips

* Keep your knees bent

* Keep your back straight

* Lift with your legs, not with your back

* Do not try to lift a lot at once

* Start by clearing only what is necessary for the car to pull out of the driveway

SELL IT!

Door to Door

Go from house to house in your neighborhood with flyers for your service. Ring the doorbell. If they answer, briefly introduce yourself, saying, "Hi, I'm ____, and I shovel snow in the neighborhood! Here is my contact information (hand them a flyer), and note that your first half hour is free! Please call me if I can ever be of assistance!

SALES STRATEGY

Seasonal Snow Strategy

Snow creates a storm of demand for this business during the winter season. Talk to your neighbors as winter approaches, and don't give up on selling your service until the season is over!

SUCCESSFUL KID ENTREPRENEUR
INTERVIEWS

BENJAMIN STERN

Started Nohbo at age 14

Creator of the First Eco-Friendly Shampoo Ball

Ben was inspired to make a difference when, at 14 years old, he viewed a video about the destructive impact of the plastic industry on our marine life. Ben envisioned a tab-like, single-use product that was water soluble for personal care products, such as shampoo, conditioner, body wash, and shaving cream. In early 2016, Ben appeared on ABC's "Shark Tank" to pitch his business, Nohbo, and ended up accepting a business offer from billionaire Mark Cuban.

BENJAMIN STERN

INTERVIEW With Benjamin Stern

- -

1. Did you have any business or work experience before you started your business?

Nohbo wasn't my first company. I started a coffee subscription company, selling bags of coffee I bought at wholesale prices to neighbors, using the same model as typical school sales programs do. It was a nice business, but there was a limit to how big the business could get. That's when I realized I needed to create an invention.

2. What inspired you to start your company?

Escaping a job inspired me to create my own company. I saw my parents dislike their day jobs, and personally, I did not like working for others. I always had ideas, and ever since a young age, I've heard mentors, friends, teachers, etc. say that America was a place where opportunity exists for everyone. The word "everyone" does not have an age attached, so I saw my opportunity, had this amazing chance to grow it, and boom; my company was created.

3. What were the first steps that you took in starting your business?

The first step was to make sure others found my shampoo ball appealing. I did this by submitting the concept to companies like The Clorox Company and Hyatt Hotels. Following their positive reaction, I jumped on the idea and decided to turn this concept from nothing into a rolling stone. The next steps were finding legal counsel, saving up money, finding chemists, and just working out all the additional kinks in forming a startup.

4. What was your biggest challenge in starting a business?

I believe the biggest challenge in starting a business is, well, starting a business. Having an idea DOES NOT make you a business. Taking the first steps—like forming a legal company, building a website, and finding your base—makes you a business (...). In the beginning, you may have little to no emotional support, and through that process, you may be discouraged from continuing. It is commonly known that around 9 out of 10 startups fail. I don't believe that statistic; I think it's more like 9 out of 10 startups with some who really never started up, fail.

5. Do you have any advice for aspiring kid/teen entrepreneurs?

One of my favorite quotes is "He who hesitates is lost." Get up, create something cool, and never be discouraged by unknowledgeable people who have no idea what they're saying or doing! Only one person will make you who you want to be: you.

6. Was there any one decision that was truly key to your company's success?

Yes, building a strong team full of experts in their field has allowed the company to grow best. I was in a position where I could continue to hog some of the control, or give it to those who knew what they were doing better in their specific fields, so in order for me to avoid a certain mistake, they make decisions. Allowing others to make decisions has helped alleviate some of the stress from not only my shoulders, but everyone's.

7. If you could go back in time and make one change to your business, what would it be?
I believe the biggest change I would make is learning to prioritize better, so we would be in a position to invest more in research and development before getting ahead of ourselves. Growing slow is good, but too slow will allow your competitors to catch on and pass you.

8. What do you want to be when you grow up?
I consider myself grown up, and am doing what I want to be doing. Maybe I'll expand my field and expertise in the ever changing tech world, but I want to be running a business. I don't see myself retiring, even if I get to the point where I never need another dime for me or my family to live. This has turned into a game, and I just plain out love it.

9. What have you learned through starting and running your business?
I have learned a lot, but I think the number one lesson is don't lose your drive. For a while, business owners will be working for their company, nurturing it like a baby, to get it off the ground. It is hard, scratch that, this isn't hard. The beauty of what we do is it is something anyone can do; it can be very time consuming, tedious, tiresome, and at many times, just plain discouraging work, but I wouldn't describe it as hard. Anyways, you need something to be driving you to keep that excitement you first experienced when you thought of the idea and were encouraged to push it out to the public. Money is often an appealing end result, and I firmly believe it could be that driving force, but shouldn't be the only one. Think of what you are selling, and just enjoy the moments when a customer comes back with appreciation for what you've done. On a side note, never believe the myth that this will be fun all the time. It is an amazing experience nonetheless.

10. Why should fellow kids and teens start their own businesses?
Why not? You could succeed, and have experience, money, and even more opportunities, or you could fail, and still have experience and more opportunities than your peers. They say if one is under 35 years old, they can ALWAYS reaccumulate wealth to where it was. But for kids and teens, we have it even better. A house won't be foreclosed on us, a creditor won't be seeking a return, and we will always wake up and go to bed with food on our plates and a house over our head. Kids don't have to worry nearly as much about living expenses, which makes it a golden time to start.

ANDREA CAO
Started Q-Flex at age 13
Creator of the Leading Self-Acupressure Device

Andrea Cao is a 16 year old CEO, entrepreneur, and horse trainer. She's been featured on Shark Tank, Beyond the Tank, Buzzfeed, Forbes, QVC, FOX, ABC, Inc., and Business Insider. She has become the youngest entrepreneur to host on QVC, and the youngest to have executive meetings at Walmart. Andrea is a hustling businesswoman by day and an avid equestrian by night.

INTERVIEW With Andrea Cao

1. Did you have any business or work experience before you started your business?
As a 13 year old, I couldn't really say that I had much work or business experience prior to starting Q-Flex. Looking back, however, I noticed that I really was born an entrepreneur. I had started all kinds of small businesses here and there, including selling live frogs and lizards to classmates, custom horse shampoo, and even my own line of trading cards. And that was just the beginning of it! While none of this generated much money, it fueled my spark and gave me priceless experiences that really set me up for starting my first "real" business.

2. What inspired you to start your company?
I was inspired to invent the Q-Flex when my mom would always come home with a sore back from work. I hated seeing her in pain and I couldn't really do much to help. I thought about how many other people must be suffering from the same issue, and as a joke, I told myself, "Why don't I make something to fix that?" Well, if you knew 13-year-old Andrea, you would know that if she wants something, she works to make it happen. So what started out as a joke turned into a design on paper, which turned into a prototype, and eventually turned into an actual product!

3. What were the first steps that you took in starting your business?
After I had my first finished product in my hands, I did anything and everything I could to get the product out there. As a 13-year-old with essentially no formal marketing training or experience, it was quite the challenge. But, with high hopes I set out selling and pitching my product door to door, with each pitch getting stronger and me getting more confident! I became quite the saleswoman after those experiences, and those pitch skills landed me with deals in local health and fitness stores!

4. What was your biggest challenge in starting a business?
I would have to say that my biggest challenge at first was the age gap. I quickly shoved myself into a grown-up industry, and was often not taken seriously in the beginning. I had to say goodbye to the comforts of childhood and step into the real, intimidating world with big words and terms that I didn't quite understand. It pushed me to learn how to be comfortable when I'm the odd one out, which is something that I am super grateful for today.

5. Do you have any advice for aspiring kid/teen entrepreneurs?
You do you. Don't listen to the world telling you the big lie of "You can't." As an entrepreneur, you have to push yourself out of your comfort zone and learn to go against the grain. I am a firm believer that if you want something bad enough, you'll find a way, and if not, you'll find excuses. You control how much effort you put forth, and it's going to reflect in your business and attitude, good or bad.

When (not if) you fall, you get back up to see why you fell and how you can do better next time. Everything is a learning experience, so take advantage of it. And always remember that there are always going to be people seemingly more experienced, older, smarter, richer, etc., than you, but a river cuts through rock because of its persistence, not its power.

6. Was there any one decision that was truly key to your company's success?
Partnering with Mark Cuban and Barbara Corcoran on Shark Tank was huge. They took my business from a little girl going door to door and helped me turn it in to a million dollar, internationally recognized company. Both of them have taught me so many key lessons and values that I will use for the rest of my life.

7. If you could go back in time and make one change to your business, what would it be?
Honestly, I don't think I'd change a thing! I truly believe that this journey played out exactly how it was supposed to, and everything I've received (good or bad) has been a blessing that I am thankful for every day.

8. What do you want to be when you grow up?
As of now, I am a horse trainer and business owner, and I intend to keep it that way. I train wild mustangs, problem horses, and performance horses on my ranch as horses are my passion. I eventually want to start some equine companies because I know the market and the consumer very well (I am one haha!). I know that the moment I turn 18, I'm getting my real estate license so I can invest in some rental homes and properties, because I love real estate.

9. What have you learned through starting and running your business?
Running my businesses has taught me too much to list in a couple of sentences, but to sum it up, I would have to say it has taught me a lot about life in general. I have developed so many key values and learnings which I know I will use my whole life. I have learned how to prioritize my time, manage my money, take calculated risks, and that's just the beginning of it. I have developed a strong work ethic, and an entrepreneurial mindset that sets me up for success. I know how to be independent and self-reliant to get things done myself.

10. Why should fellow kids and teens start their own businesses?
Starting your own business is the best decision you can make as a kid or teen. It'll teach you much more than you could ever learn in a classroom and make you a driven, strong, and awesome individual. Just like horses, a lot of young people need a job or a goal. If you find what you're passionate about and put your mind to it, you will go so far in life. Entrepreneurs are a different breed that live on different terms, and when we want something, we stop at nothing to get it. I can't think of anything more empowering than starting your own business and sticking with it. And who knows, you might even make some good money while you're at it.

KATIE OSHINS

Started at age 11

KObracelets, a Charitable Fashion Company

Katie spends her time learning, dancing, playing tennis, hanging out with her friends, and watching Netflix. Her favorite show is Grey's Anatomy which, along with her work for St. Jude, has inspired her to pursue medicine in the future.

INTERVIEW With Katie Oshins

1. Did you have any business or work experience before you started your business?
Yes, in 3rd grade I created a business also, in fact, for St. Jude's Children Hospital. I made duct tape bows and headbands and sold them. In the end I raised over $800 and donated all of the proceeds.

2. What inspired you to start your company?
Also in 3rd grade, I read a book written by Patricia Palacco, *The Lemonade Club*. It was about a whole class shaving their heads for a student who suffered with cancer. This really inspired me to help others in a way that the class did; however, I wasn't quite up to shaving my head at the time.

3. What were the first steps that you took in starting your business?
I asked myself three questions: 1. What am I good at? 2. What do I enjoy doing? 3. What is something a consumer would want? Once I settled on an idea, I made several prototypes and researched cost of materials. I also had to set up a time management plan so I could keep up with school and still have a social life.

4. What was your biggest challenge in starting a business?
My biggest struggle would probably be getting the word out about KObracelets. Once I had the product completed, how was I supposed to sell it? I went around the neighborhood selling them, utilized my family and friends, hosted jewelry parties to promote KObracelets, and marketed through social media. After the buzz got out, someone offered to collaborate with me and create a website.

5. Do you have any advice for aspiring kid/teen entrepreneurs?
I'd tell them when starting a business, do something that touches you and that you would enjoy. That way, you will have the motivation to keep going during hard times.

6. Was there any one decision that was truly key to your company's success?
Yes, creating a website that allowed me to reach out to people beyond my geographical location. Suddenly, I was being flooded with orders from various locations all around the world, such as New York, Florida, Australia, and Singapore.

7. If you could go back in time and make one change to your business, what would it be?
Honestly, though there were many challenges, I wouldn't change a thing at this point in the business. While there were tough decisions that had to be made, it was those decisions that taught me the most about entrepreneurship.

8. What do you want to be when you grow up?
I aspire to become a surgeon. I have always been interested in the medical field and would love to save the lives of more people one day.

9. What have you learned through starting and running your business?
I have learned that it takes a lot of perseverance, grit, and commitment in order to stick to the path you created for yourself. There will always be struggles and problems, but it's overcoming them that's key to success.

10. Why should fellow kids and teens start their own businesses?
Not only is it a great experience for the "real world," but in doing so, one feels accomplished and proud of who they have become. Some of the best feelings in the world are gratitude and pride. In addition, one is put in numerous situations in which they may have to step out of their comfort zones. This leads to tremendous growth.

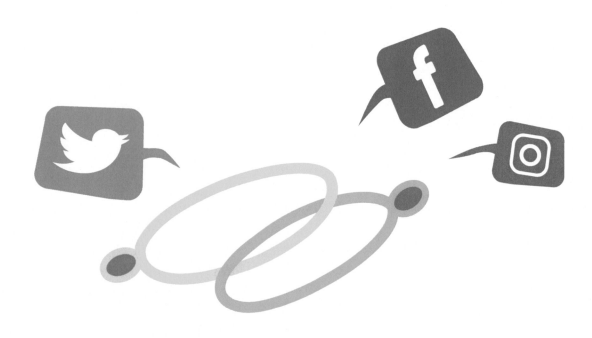

TAHOE MACK
Started at age 14
CatchingYourDreamz, an Etsy art store

Tahoe has always loved personalization and self-expression, which is what inspired her to start her etsy shop. The art community motivated her to think outside the box and to make the world her own. She hopes to inspire young girls and boys to work towards being the best versions of themselves.

INTERVIEW With Tahoe Mack

1. Did you have any business or work experience before you started your business?
Prior to creating my business I literally had no idea about entrepreneurship.

2. What inspired you to start your company?
Art has always inspired me to create different ways of expression, so I truely wanted to create something that individuals could use to show off there uniqueness!

3. What were the first steps that you took in starting your business?
First, I came up with an initial, broad plan. I wanted to make and sell dream catchers.

4. What was your biggest challenge in starting a business?
My biggest challenge was setting a correct price. Make sure you budget your time and pay yourself for hard work!

5. Do you have any advice for aspiring kid/teen entrepreneurs?
If you really want to accomplish something, big or small, don't limit yourself with negativity. If you create a clear path toward your dreams nothing can stand in your way!

6. Was there any one decision that was truly key to your company's success?
A turning point for my store was when I decided to branch off and create stickers. It was a huge step in a different direction but without it I may have not had my Etsy store today.

7. If you could go back in time and make one change to your business, what would it be?
I wish I had created more variations and gone even more in depth with my dreamcatchers.

8. What do you want to be when you grow up?
When I grow up, I want to own my own company that involves the art community.

9. What have you learned through starting and running your business?
I learned a lot about myself and what I am capable of. It gave me a lot of confidence in my ideas which pushes me forward every day.

10. Why should fellow kids and teens start their own businesses?
Starting your own business really puts you ahead of the game. It gives you not only the opportunity to experience the pleasure of self-reliance but also helps you understand how the economy works.

EXTRA CONTENT

EXTRA:
Make Money in Your Sleep

Trading your time for money will never lead to real money. You only have 8,760 hours in a year, and much of that is spent sleeping. You must set up businesses that continue to make money even when you sleep. Making money while you are not working is the key to real money.

Doctors, lawyers, engineers, and many others are highly skilled professionals, trading time for money. But there is a limit on the money they can earn. That limit is the number of hours that they can work. It can be so much easier to make money in your sleep!

The good news about making money while you sleep is that it is easier than ever because of the Internet. Fifty years ago, making money while you sleep was difficult. To build a business, you needed to have a building and were limited by location and hours. Now, the Internet makes it almost free to open a store that's open 24 hours a day to billions of customers around the world. The Internet has made it easier than ever to make money in your sleep.

Practice

It's your turn to practice this. Even though your first business might not sell stuff online, one day you will likely want to start a business that sells items on the Internet. This will open up the door for people around the world to be able to buy your stuff. Two places you might want to sell your items first are eBay or Etsy, since they make it really easy to set up an online store.

In the space below, write some ides for stuff that you would like to sell online. Using the Internet to sell your items online will be the easiest way for you to start making money in your sleep. It may be 2:00 in the morning, but the duct tape wallet that you are selling on Etsy might still sell online. That is why the Internet is so amazing!

PRODUCTS & SERVICES TO SELL ONLINE

1 --

2 --

3 --

4 --

5 --

6 --

7 --

8 --

9 --

10 --

EXTRA:
Legal Tips

Disclosure: This is not professional legal advice. We highly recommend talking to a small business attorney in your community.

* It is rare that a minor (someone under 18 years old) can form a legal entity

* Parents will likely want to structure the company as a sole proprietorship (the cheapest method) and then pay their kid its profits as an allowance

* A sole proprietorship with a business name will typically be required to file for a DBA, which stands for "doing business as"

* Most businesses require a variety of business permits and/or licenses to operate legally

* Sellers of products and services may need to collect and pay a tax, such as a sales tax

* Profits will likely be subject to taxation

* Don't know where to start? Here are three great resources for small business owners:

    » The Small Business Administration:
       howanykidcanstartabusiness.com/sba-start

    » LegalZoom or RocketLawyer:
       howanykidcanstartabusiness.com/legalzoom-start
       howanykidcanstartabusiness.com/rocketlawyer-start

    » Local small business attorneys

Acknowledgements

We would like to thank Lorena Molinari for her excellent illustrations throughout the book, Imran Shaikh for his illustration of the cover, and Danielle Lincoln Hanna for her excellent work in serving as our children's book editor.

We would also like to express appreciation to Shayna Indyg for her photos and guide in "Scented Soaps," Nick Tehle, Iris Weisman, and Iris' son Brad for contributions to "Car Wash Craze," and Atri for his contribution to "Water Bottles."

We especially appreciate Camille McCue, Blythe Cherney, Kendal Martin, Robin Oshins, Rachel Ziter, and the students of the Adelson Educational Campus for their input on an advance copy of the book, as well as Victoria Lopez, Skarlett Severson, Dylan Kai Hasimoto, Alexander Matthew Caday, Sahil Bhatnagar, Devika Bhatnagar, Ailla Nancarrow, Isabel Dorado-gentry, Zara Pehlivani, Farah Purewal, Kaiya Elle Kakita, and Skylar Segovia for taking the time to attend and provide feedback in a focus group setting.

Made in the USA
San Bernardino, CA
05 June 2017